1

SHINY AND HER WARDROBE OF VIRTUES

GRATITUDE

THE FEELING OF BEING THANKFUL

BY

Sukanya Shah

BIRCH
BOOKS

First published by Birch Books 2020

ISBN - 978-81-949495-0-3

Email : books.birch@gmail.com

To Adyana.
My first. My all.
May you always be more.

From the Author's Desk

Cossetted in our homes during the thick of the Covid-19 pandemic, I made every effort to keep my toddler happy and engaged. It made me wonder about the true legacy in learning that my child will bequeath. I cannot wait to pass on this treasure of a less than perfect world to her… one that will astonish her most often, teach her most definitely and hold her to two constants—challenge and change.

Shiny And Her Wardrobe Of Virtues was born of this sentiment. Shiny is a spritely little girl who owns a magical wardrobe, with virtuous items that on adorning, change her world view…virtues that go beyond the classroom and make her feel happy and whole.

I enjoyed writing these stories of gratitude, kindness, confidence, patience and love…but more so, I enjoyed diving into these most beautiful emotions and feelings with my child.

I hope you do too.

Love,
Sukanya.

It was a bright Monday morning in Virtueville,
Shiny woke up feeling fresh and thrilled.

She saw the golden sun, she felt the moist dew,
Mummy called out, she heard the kettle brew.

The first day of big school, it was a special day,
She got dressed in her best, eager to learn and play.

She peered into her wardrobe, with its clothes and shoes grand,
A magical green coat of gratitude, she felt with her hand.

It was shimmery and silky, and fit just right,
In her green coat of gratitude, Shiny was a sight!

She gobbled up her breakfast, it tasted so yummy,
The coat started shimmering, as she said "thank you, mummy".

Off Shiny went, on the school bus cheerily,
She felt so thankful, her heart beat with glee.

She loved her new class, and her new teacher so polite,
"Hello, dear friends," she exclaimed in sheer delight!

The first lesson was English,
Shiny loved it best,
She learned a big new word, the
big new word was 'blessed'.

Blessed

"Do you know what blessed means?", asked the teacher curiously, "It means to be watched over, and feel lucky endlessly!"

The words came out of Shiny, as her coat glistened green,
How was she so clever? Was it all but a dream?

GRATITUDE

"Let's be thankful today, dear children of grade one".
"As you go along, you'll see, gratitude is fun".

"Let's start by saying thanks, for this world we live in",
"For this healthy body and mind, and that happy little grin."

"What are you thankful for?", asked the teacher to the class.
"For the rainbows, the moon and stars... for the meadows and the flowers."

"We're thankful for our food", said Shiny from the front row,
"For delicious fruits and vegetables and the lofty trees that grow."

"We're thankful for our homes", exclaimed Shiny loudly,
"For warm hugs and kisses from Mummy and Daddy!"

This grand, green coat of gratitude made Shiny so thankful,
She felt her heart swell, feeling happy and full.

Happy
Wow
Guided
Thank you

To be grateful is to know, how very blessed you are,
To say a thank you prayer, as you wish upon a star.

This grand, green gratitude coat made Shiny see,
How being thankful was her chance, to be the very best kind of "me".

Talking points for parents:

- Ask your child what they feel thankful or blessed for?
- Tell your child how grateful you are to be their parents and what about them you appreciate and love.
- Prompt your child to say 'thank you' more often through the day.
- Start a morning or nighttime routine of telling your child what you are grateful for and ask them the same in return.

RECAP

Fill the bubbles with your feelings when you read the story.